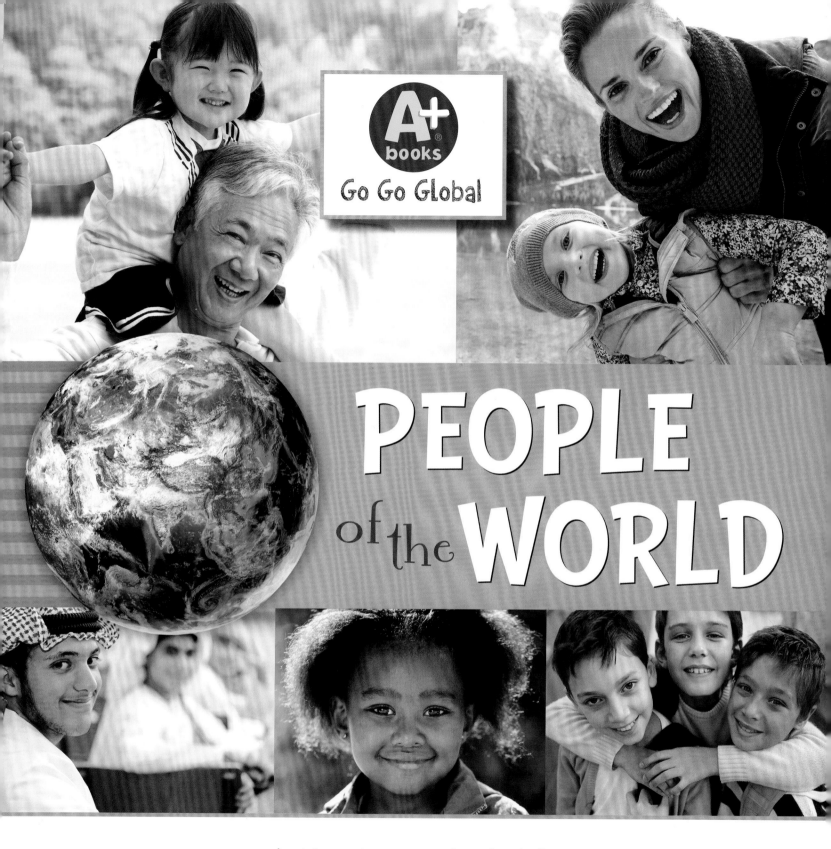

PEOPLE of the WORLD

by Nancy Loewen and Paula Skelley

CAPSTONE PRESS
a capstone imprint

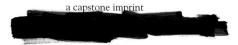

Look in the mirror.

United States

Whose face do you see?

France

You see **you** and
I see **me.**

Every face is special.

China

Nicaragua

Indonesia

Brazil

Every face **belongs.**

Lebanon

Canada

Thailand

6

Ghana

Our **faces** tell a **story** ...

Madagascar

Jamaica

so say it **loud** and **strong!**

Madagascar

Your eyes may be **brown.**

Philippines

Finland

Your eyes may be **blue**.

But **each day**
they **open** to
a **world** that's
new.

India

A smile says, "Hello."

Malaysia

England

Egypt

Russia

Cuba

Germany

A smile says,
"Good-bye."

A **smile** says, "I love you."

United States

A **smile** says,

"I'll try."

Vietnam

We use our **hands** to

do, do, **do** ...

Thailand

to **sew** a **dress**

Sweden

or **make** a **stew.**

Write

Bolivia

or **play.**

Argentina

20

Plant

England

or **pray.**

Our
hands
keep **busy**
every day.

India

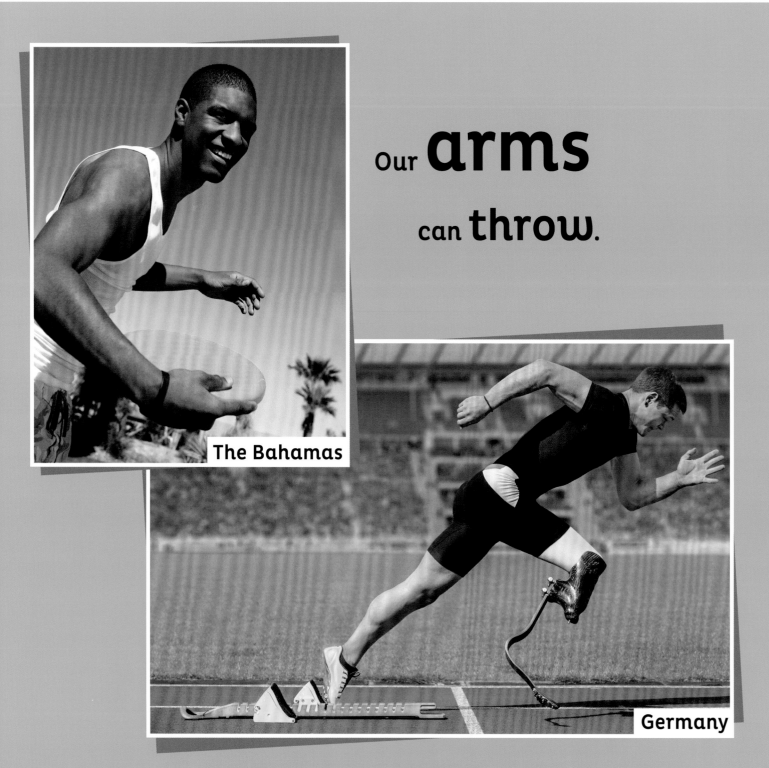

Our **arms** can **throw**.

The Bahamas

Germany

Our **legs** can **run**.

South Africa

Our **feet** can **dance.**

England

Let's have some fun!

United States

Thailand

New Zealand

Canada

We start life
small ...

Brazil

Tanzania

26

United States

then **grow** and **grow**.

China

we **change**
the
world ...

Greece

Vietnam

wherever
we go!

NORTH
AMERICA

Canada

United
States

The Bahamas
Cuba
Jamaica
Nicaragua

SOUTH
AMERICA

Bolivia   Brazil

Argentina

EUROPE

Finland
Sweden
England   Germany
France

Greece
Lebanon

Egypt

AFRICA

Ghana

Tanzania

Madagascar

Botswana

South
Africa

ANTARCTICA

Russia

ASIA

China

India

Thailand — Vietnam
Philippines

— Malaysia

Indonesia

AUSTRALIA

New Zealand

GLOSSARY

mirror—a smooth, shiny surface that shows the image of the person or thing in front of it

pray—to speak to God or a god to give thanks or to ask for help

sew—to make, repair, or fasten something with a needle and thread

stew—a dish made of vegetables and meat or fish cooked together in a liquid

CRITICAL THINKING USING THE COMMON CORE

1. What do all of the people in this book have in common? (Key Ideas and Details)

2. Name four things in this book that people around the world may do with their hands. (Key Ideas and Details)

3. Which smiles in this book are most like yours? Which smiles are most unlike yours? How are they different? (Integration of Knowledge and Ideas)

A+ Books are published by Capstone Press,
1710 Roe Crest Drive, North Mankato, Minnesota 56003
www.capstonepub.com

Library of Congress Cataloging-in-Publication Data
Cataloging-in-publication information is on file with the Library of Congress.
ISBN 978-1-4914-3920-3 (library binding)
ISBN 978-1-4914-3931-9 (paperback)
ISBN 978-1-4914-3941-8 (eBook PDF)

Editorial Credits
Jill Kalz, editor; Juliette Peters, designer; Tracy Cummins, media researcher; Tori Abraham, production specialist

Photo Credits
Dreamstime: Alessio Moiola, 26 BL, Konstantin Shevtsov, 14 BL, Sjors737, 20 Top, Woraphon Banchobdi, 25 TR; Getty Images: Asiaselects, 2, Mark D Phillips, 23; iStockphoto: bo1982, 28 Top, Britta Kasholm-Tengve, 26 BR, Casarsa, 20 Bottom, IPGGutenbergUKLtd, 22 Top; Shutterstock: Aleksandar Todorovic, 14 BR, Alliance, 1 TR, Anton_Ivanov, Cover BR, Banana Republic images, 6 BR, berna namoglu, 15, Blend Images, 25 TL, bonga1965, 5 TR, Digital Media Pro, 24, dome, 14 TR, dr322, 8, 10 Top, Filipe Frazao, 5 Bottom, frantab, 17, John Bill, 29, karelnoppe, 1 BM, 14 TL, KOMISAR, 3, leocalvett, Cover, 1 (globe), Lucian Coman, 16, luckypic, 21 Top, mezzotint, 22 Bottom, MidoSemsem, 14 Middle, Monkey Business Images, Cover Back, 1 TL, Natalia Dobryanskaya, 28 Bottom, Naypong, 18, Patryk Kosmider, Cover TL, photoff, Cover TR, Praisaeng, 19 Top, Pressmaster, 1 BR, Rawpixel, 25 Bottom, riekephotos, 6 BL, rj lerich, 5 TL, Ruslan Guzov, 27, Shyamalamuralinath, 21 Bottom, Solis Images, 19 Bottom, spyx, 10 Bottom, stawek, 30 TL , Sura Nualpradid, 7, szefei, 4, 12, testing, Cover BL, uliaLine, 11, ZouZou, 1 BL, Zurijeta, 6 Top; SuperStock: age fotostock, 9, 26 Top.

READ MORE

Diaz, Natalia. *A Ticket Around the World.* Berkeley, Calif.: Owlkids Books, Inc., 2015.

Kerley, Barbara. *One World, One Day.* Washington, D.C.: National Geographic, 2009.

Lewis, Clare. *Families Around the World.* Around the World. Chicago: Heinemann Library, 2015.

INTERNET SITES

FactHound offers a safe, fun way to find Internet sites related to this book. All of the sites on FactHound have been researched by our staff.

Here's all you do:
Visit *www.facthound.com*
Type in this code:
9781491439203

Check out projects, games and lots more at
www.capstonekids.com